Food Webs

Who Eats What?

Claire Llewellyn

Raintree

Chicago, Illinois

© 2014 Heinemann Library
an imprint of Capstone Global Library, LLC
Chicago, Illinois

To contact Capstone Global Library please call 800-747-4992, or visit our web site www.capstonepub.com

Edited by Adam Miller, Sian Smith, and Penny West
Designed by Philippa Jenkins
Original illustrations © Capstone Global Library Ltd 2014
Illustrated by Oxford Designers and Illustrators, and Words and Publications
Picture research by Tracy Cummins
Originated by Capstone Global Library Ltd
Produced by Victoria Fitzgerald
Printed and bound in China by CTPS

17 16 15 14 13
10 9 8 7 6 5 4 3 2 1

Library of Congress Cataloging-in-Publication Data
Llewellyn, Claire.
  Food webs : who eats what? / Claire Llewellyn.
     pages cm.—(Show me science)
  Includes bibliographical references and index.
  ISBN 978-1-4329-8750-3 (hardback)—ISBN 978-1-4329-8757-2 (paperback) 1. Food chains (Ecology)—Juvenile literature. 2. Predation (Biology)—Juvenile literature. I. Title.

QH541.14.L58 2014
577'.16—dc23   2013013124

Acknowledgments
The author and publisher are grateful to the following for permission to reproduce copyright material:
Getty Images pp. 4 (bmse), 7 (FLPA), 9 (Luis Javier Sandoval), 14 (Werner Bollmann), 20 (Thomas Marent), 21 (Thomas Kitchin & Victoria Hurst), 23 (J. Sneesby/B. Wilkins), 24 (Panoramic Images), 26 (Visuals Unlimited), 28 (Cesar Ed), 29 (David Yarrow Photography); Shutterstock pp. 11 (© Vishnevskiy Vasily), 12 (© Steve Byland), 13 (© Stephen Rees), 17 bottom (© Borislav Borisov), 22 (© wim claes), 25 (© Rich Carey), 27 (© Dirk Ercken); Superstock pp. 5 (Animals Animals), 15 (imagebroker.net), 16 (age footstock), 17 top (Animals Animals), 18 (Michael S. Nolan / age footstock), 19 (FLPA).

Cover photograph of Great Crested Flycatcher (Myiarchus crinitus) with dragonfly prey in its beak, Pennsylvania reproduced with permission of Getty Images (Visuals Unlimited, Inc./Joe McDonald).

We would like to thank Michael Bright for his invaluable help in the preparation of this book.

Contents

Food for Life 4

A Chain of Food 6

Building a Web 8

It Starts with a Plant 10

Feeding on Plants 12

Designed to Hunt 14

Competing for Food 16

Hunting Together 18

Beware of the Trap! 20

Staying Alive 22

Safety in Numbers 24

Tricking the Enemy 26

Keeping a Balance 28

Glossary 30

Find Out More 31

Index 32

Some words are shown in bold, **like this**. You can find out what they mean by looking in the glossary.

Food for Life

A chipmunk scampers over the ground, searching for nuts, berries, and seeds. A hawk flies in the sky above. Hawks are **predators** and have very sharp eyes. This bird spots the chipmunk and dives down swiftly to snatch its **prey**. It kills the chipmunk with its long, sharp talons then tears it open with its sharp, hooked beak.

The need for food

All animals need food, whether it is seeds, berries, or juicy flesh. Food provides **energy** to keep the body working. It also supplies **nutrients**—the building blocks that the body needs to grow and repair itself.

A hawk hangs in the air, its eyes fixed on its prey. Soon it will dive for the kill.

Capuchin monkeys eat bananas and other kinds of fruit.

Animals eat whatever they can find in their **habitat**. Many feed only on plants, some feed only on meat, and others eat a mixture of the two. Feeding is so important that, over millions of years, predators have gained skills and weapons that help them to hunt. Prey animals do not want to be eaten, so they have gained defenses. Some, such as chipmunks, defend themselves by living in burrows under the ground.

This book looks at what animals eat. It looks at the battle between predators and prey—how hunters try to catch a meal and how their "meals" do their best to survive.

A change of diet

Giant pandas eat bamboo. Yet, by studying their **digestive system**, scientists can tell that in the past these animals once ate meat. Pandas must have changed their diet in order to survive.

A Chain of Food

When a barn owl catches a shrew, it has a meal that provides **energy** and **nutrients**.

Q: Where have the nutrients and energy come from?

A: They came from the slugs and other animals that the shrew ate.

Q: But where did their nutrients and energy come from?

A: They came from the plants that the beetles and slugs ate.

Q: And where did those nutrients and energy come from?

A: The energy came from the Sun. The plants made use of the Sun's energy and grew roots, stems, leaves, and fruits. These contain valuable nutrients.

Energy passes from the Sun to the owl through a chain of nutrients. This is called a food chain.

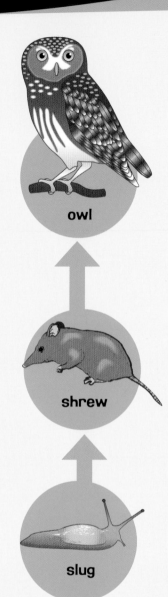

owl

shrew

slug

plants

the Sun

A successful barn owl carries a shrew to a safe place where it can feed.

Links in the chain

The nutrients plants contain are passed on through a chain of animals. First they pass to plant-eating animals, which are known as **herbivores**. Then they pass to meat-eating animals, known as **carnivores**. There are always fewer carnivores than plant-eating animals. If there were more carnivores, they would eventually wipe out the animals they feed on. At the top of the food chain are **species** like the barn owl that no animal feeds on. These are known as **apex predators**.

RECYCLING NUTRIENTS

When plants and animals die, their bodies are broken down by fungi, worms, and other **decomposers**. The nutrients contained in the rotting remains eventually mix with the soil. This makes the soil more fertile and helps new plants to grow.

Building a Web

All plants and animals are linked into food chains. Food chains contain different **species**, but they always build from plants at the bottom to large **predators** at the top. The food chains in a **habitat** connect to form a feeding web of links. This is called a food web.

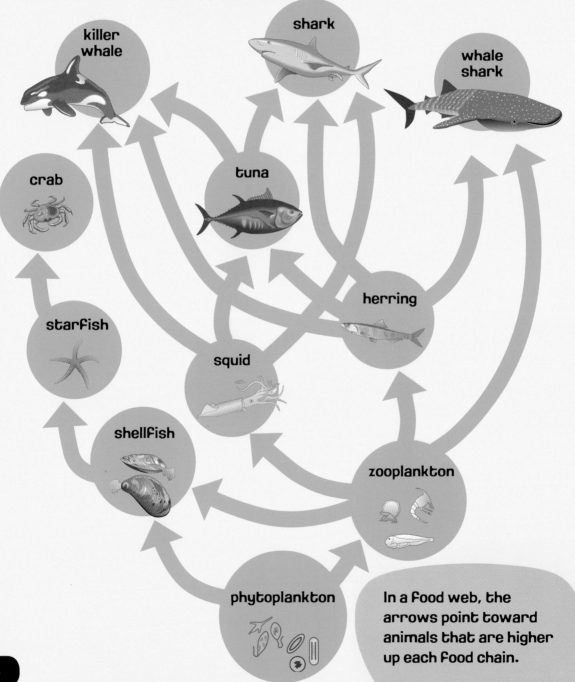

In a food web, the arrows point toward animals that are higher up each food chain.

The whale shark

From tip to tail, a whale shark is roughly as big as a bus. It swims along with its mouth open, scooping up huge mouthfuls of water. The water passes through filters in its throat, and any food that gets trapped is gulped down.

An ocean food web

The open ocean is a vast habitat with a huge variety of food chains. They start with tiny plantlike living things called **phytoplankton**. They make their own food using the Sun's **energy**.

Phytoplankton are food for microscopic creatures known as **zooplankton**, such as baby shrimps and crabs. Zooplankton are food for many animals—from herring to whale sharks, the largest fish in the sea.

Many sea creatures hunt one another. Some, such as jellyfish, simply catch food as it drifts by. Others, such as sharks, hunt using their senses and powerful bodies. The largest, strongest animals are **apex** predators.

The diagram of an ocean food web on page 8 shows only the main parts of an animal's diet. For example, sharks feed on many kinds of **prey**, but their main foods are fish and squid.

It Starts with a Plant

Food chains and food webs would never get started without plants. Plants get the ball rolling. They do not need to eat other things because they can make food for themselves.

Making food

A plant's leaves work like a food factory. They take **energy** from the Sun and a gas called carbon dioxide from the air. They mix these with water to make a sweet, starchy food. This important process is called **photosynthesis**. The food it produces gives the plant energy and **nutrients** to live and grow. The plant can now make new roots, stems, leaves, buds, flowers, fruits, and seeds.

leaves soak up sunlight

water and carbon dioxide mix in the leaves to make a sweet, starchy food

carbon dioxide enters the leaves from the air

A healthy plant can grow and feed itself, using sunlight, air, water, and nutrients.

water and nutrients are taken in by roots

10

A strong foundation

Plants are the foundation stone of life on Earth. If plants did not grow, **herbivores** would have nothing to eat. The **predators** that feed on them would starve, too.

Waxwings feed on the berries of the hawthorn tree.

Produce or consume?

Animals cannot make food for themselves. They have to find it. Herbivores, such as horses and field mice, feed on plants. **Carnivores**, such as foxes and owls, hunt and feed on herbivores.

Plants are known as food **producers** because they produce food that others can eat. Animals consume this food, so they are known as **consumers**.

Feeding on Plants

The food that plants make for themselves is also good for animals. This is why so many **species** feed on plants: green turtles tear up sea grass, groundhogs gnaw roots, butterflies feed on **nectar**, and toucans feed on fruit.

Tools for the job

In many cases, an animal's body has **adaptations** to help it feed. The giraffe's long neck allows it to eat the softest leaves at the top of a tree. Other animals cannot reach this high, so giraffes always have plenty to eat. Hummingbirds are adapted, too. They have long, fine beaks, which they use like drinking straws to suck up the nectar from inside flowers.

A hummingbird beats its wings very quickly to hover as it feeds from flowers. The sweet nectar works as a fuel, to give it the **energy** it needs.

Keep off!

Some plants have tough defenses to stop animals from eating them. Brambles have sharp thorns. Nettles have a painful sting. Milkweed contains a poisonous white liquid that can kill horses, cattle, and sheep.

Hidden benefits

You might think being eaten is a big problem for plants. After all, if an animal eats too much of it, a plant will probably die. Yet there can be benefits for the plant. When hummingbirds feed on flowers, they spread the yellow **pollen** that helps plants to make seeds. When toucans feed on fruit, they carry ripe seeds to new places where the seeds can sprout and grow.

Designed to Hunt

Predators must catch every meal they eat. They must also compete with other predators in the search for **prey**. In many cases, their bodies have **adapted** to give them a helping hand.

Hunting on grasslands

The cheetah is the fastest predator on land and its body is built for speed. It has long legs, a flexible spine, a large heart to pump oxygen, and claws to grip the ground.

A cheetah's incredible stretch and speed help it to hunt down a young gazelle.

A woodpecker feeds on grubs in the bark, using its claws and tail for balance.

Hunting in trees

Woodpeckers feed on beetle grubs that live under tree bark. The birds have sharp hearing to listen for the grubs and a strong beak to drill a hole in the wood. They also have a long, sticky tongue to dip inside the tree and grab the grub.

TONGUE-TIED

A woodpecker's tongue is so long that, when it is not in use, it is wrapped around the inside of the bird's skull. In some **species**, the tongue curls around the inside of the eye socket!

Hunting at night

Bats hunt for insects at night. To find a meal in complete darkness, bats send out a stream of squeaks. They listen for the echoes that bounce back from insects in the air. Bats can tell how far away a moth is by the time it takes an echo to return. This amazing method of hunting is known as **echolocation**.

Competing for Food

Predators compete with one another for **prey**. To avoid going hungry and fighting over food, animals of the same **species** often spread out and keep to their own hunting area. This area is called their **territory**. Animals guard their territory and use a variety of signals to warn off intruders.

At sunrise, gibbons make loud, whooping calls that travel through the forest.

Morning call

Gibbons live in family groups in the rain forests of Southeast Asia. They stay inside a large territory, feeding on fruit, leaves, flowers, bark, insects, eggs, and birds. In order to avoid competing with other gibbons, they sing loudly every morning. Their beautiful calls carry several miles.

A wolf pack leader sprays a tree with his personal scent. This keeps rival wolf packs away.

Sound and scent

A wolf pack guards a large territory to ensure a steady supply of prey. Pack members howl loudly to communicate with others exactly where the boundary of their territory lies. The pack leader also marks the boundary with a strong-smelling scent.

Red for danger

A robin uses its bright red breast to flash a "Keep out!" signal to others. It also sings loudly all year round to keep trespassers at bay. If a robin's warnings fail, it will fight to the death to defend its precious patch.

SEEING RED

European robins are fierce birds. If they see a patch of red, they will go on the attack to defend their territory. They have even attacked stuffed robins and red feathers.

17

Hunting Together

Hunting takes a lot of **energy**, and for every catch there are many failures. Some animals are **adapted** to hunt together to improve their chances of success.

Killing in a pod

Orcas, a type of dolphin, are one of the ocean's top **predators**. They feed on sea lions, seals, walruses, and fish. Orcas are intelligent animals and live in groups called pods. They have learned to communicate using sounds, such as whistles. They use clever hunting methods, which they teach to their young. One method is to seek out lone seals resting on the ice. A group of orcas will charge the ice under the water, making waves that wash their **prey** into the sea. Then together they hunt it down.

Orcas inspect the ice for seals by holding their heads above the water.

Hyenas hunt on the African grasslands in packs called clans.

Killing in a pack

Lightly built, fearless, and fast, hyenas target antelope and zebra. These animals are larger than hyenas. But working together, the pack can overpower them and quickly tear them apart. Hyenas have massive jaws and powerful teeth that can tear skin and crush bone. Their **digestive system** contains powerful acids that can deal with everything—hair, skin, bones, and even teeth!

Big-hearted hunter

For its body size, a hyena's heart is very large—about one-tenth of its body weight. (A human's is less than one-hundredth.) This gives it the power to chase its prey over long distances at up to 30 miles per hour (50 kilometers per hour).

Beware of the Trap!

Some animals are not active hunters. Instead, they lie in wait to ambush their **prey** with a surprise attack. These **predators** build clever traps or trick their prey with a surprise.

Flower power

The flower mantis lives inside orchid flowers in the rain forests of Southeast Asia. The shape and color of its body exactly matches the petals where it hides. If a butterfly visits the flower, the mantis suddenly snaps its front legs, grabs its victim, and holds it tight.

Is it an insect? Is it a flower? A mantis keeps very still on an orchid, waiting for an insect.

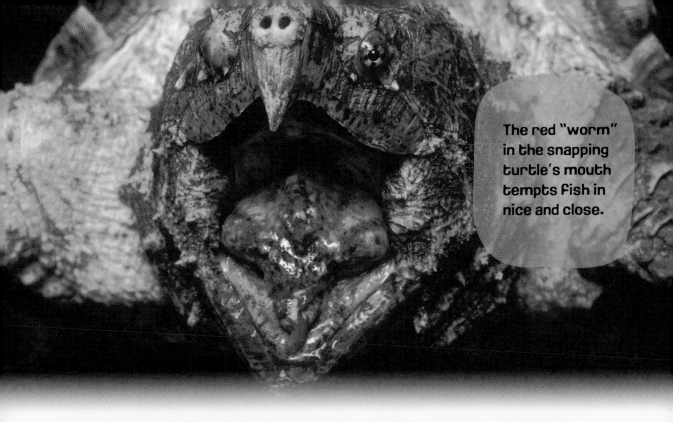

The red "worm" in the snapping turtle's mouth tempts fish in nice and close.

Is it a worm?

The alligator snapping turtle lives at the bottom of rivers and lakes. It waits with its mouth open, displaying a wriggly red tip on its tongue that gently moves in the water. To fish and frogs it looks like a worm, so they approach for a bite. Then—snap! The turtle's jaws close and it eats them instead.

Caught in a web

Spiders have lived on Earth for many millions of years. They are **adapted** to spin silk and use it to catch their insect prey—for example, by spinning a web. A spider sits quietly on its web. When an insect crashes in, the spider bites it with its **venomous** fangs and ties it up in silk.

Spider feast

The many billions of spiders on Earth eat huge numbers of insects. Scientists think that the world's spiders eat more prey, combined, than any other kind of **carnivore**.

Staying Alive

Animals that are lower down the food chain face a daily battle to survive. Over many millions of years, they have gained useful defenses that sometimes give them the edge.

Rabbit on the menu?

Rabbits are hunted by so many **predators**—owls, foxes, ferrets, stoats—that they need lots of defenses. The large eyes on the sides of their heads give them an all-around view of danger. Their strong back legs help to hurry them to safety, while their white tail flashes a warning to other rabbits nearby.

A rabbit's sharp ears warn of rustles in the grass.

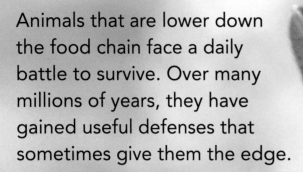

Inside a shell

Many animals have a coat of tough skin to protect them from attack. However, the tortoise has a hard shell, made of horn and bone. When danger threatens, the tortoise pulls its head and legs inside its shell. Then it sits tight until the predator goes away.

Breaking the shell

A tortoise's shell keeps out most predators, but eagles have learned how to get inside. They fly into the air, carrying their victim, and drop it from a great height to smash the shell.

Sharp spines

The porcupine is usually a peaceful **herbivore**, but it will attack when it feels in danger. Its hairy coat contains thousands of quills—long hairs that end in sharp, barbed tips. It raises its quills and uses them to threaten a predator. They cause huge pain if they enter the flesh.

This lion is right to be cautious with these porcupines: those long quills hurt!

Safety in Numbers

While many animals live alone, others live in large groups. These are harder for **predators** to attack.

Herds on the grasslands

A zebra grazing on its own is an easy target for a pride of lions. As the zebra lowers its head, it loses sight of the surrounding grasslands. This gives the predators time to creep forward. Lions need to get very close—they can only charge over a short distance. If the zebra lives in a herd, other zebras keep watch while it feeds. They snort if they see danger. At this signal, the herd runs, leaving the lions too far behind to make a successful attack.

Studying stripes

Zebras all look the same, but each animal has its own unique pattern of black and white stripes. The pattern works like a fingerprint, helping zebras to identify each other in the herd.

A swirling school makes it hard for predators to target on a single fish.

Schools in the sea

Herring are a vital link in the ocean food web. These small fish feed on **zooplankton**. In turn, they are eaten by larger animals, such as tuna, seals, and birds. Herring cannot hide from predators, so they are **adapted** to swim in huge groups called schools. The schools appear to swim as a single fish, turning at the same moment, bunching up, then darting away from the mouths of hunters. Dazzled by the silver bodies, predators find it hard to focus and often fail in their attack.

Tricking the Enemy

Prey animals have various ways of warding off an enemy. Some carry genuine weapons, while others pretend and use tricks!

With its "frill" up and its mouth wide open, this lizard clearly feels under attack.

Frills and spills

When a frilled lizard feels threatened, it raises a flap of skin around its neck. This may make the attacker think the lizard is bigger than it really is. Other lizards have different tricks. Some make their tails drop off if they are grabbed by birds. This gives them a precious second in which to escape. Their tails regrow in a few weeks.

Genuine weapons

Small animals have powerful weapons to defend themselves from attack. The skunk uses an foul-smelling spray. Bees and wasps have painful stings. The tiny poison arrow frog stores **toxins** from its diet that can kill in minutes. These animals warn **predators** of their weapons by having bright colors or stripes.

Clever trick

Some animals have no weapons, yet they have bright colors or stripes to suggest that they do. The harmless hoverfly has the same bold stripes as the stinging wasp. Birds have learned to avoid wasps, so the hoverfly's clever trick helps to reduce the chances of attack.

Small but deadly

Poison arrow frogs live in the rain forests of South America. Native tribes that live in the forest use the poison from these frogs on their blowgun darts, which are then used for hunting.

Keeping a Balance

Every day, animals low down in the food chain are killed by animals higher up. You might think the **prey** animals would get eaten to extinction. Yet this never happens. Why?

Plenty of prey

In every food chain, there are many more prey animals than there are **predators**. Take snowshoe hares, for example. They live in parts of the Arctic and are able to have large families. This supplies food for predators, such as the Canadian lynx, and also leaves plenty of hares to breed.

An unlucky snowshoe hare falls prey to a hungry lynx.

Animal numbers

Animal numbers rise and fall. In good years, when there is plenty of food, snowshoe hares have several litters. Lynx eat these, and their numbers also grow. In years when food is scarce, there are too many hares and not enough food to go around. The weaker hares have fewer young. The lynx get so hungry that they cannot breed, and their numbers also fall.

The importance of predators

Predators feed on the weak or sick, so they help to keep animal groups healthy. They also play an important part in a balanced food web. In some parts of the ocean, for example, great white sharks are the only animals to hunt seals. Without these predators, seal numbers would grow. The seals would then eat all the fish and break the food chain.

Glossary

adapt, adaptation some kind of change in a plant or animal that helps it to survive

apex top

carnivore animal that eats meat

consumer animal that feeds on plants or other animals

decomposer animal that feeds on dead plants and animals

digestive system system in the body that takes useful substances, such as sugars, fats, and proteins, out of food

echolocation way of using sound and echoes to hunt prey

energy power needed to grow, move, and live

habitat place where a plant or animal lives

herbivore animal that feeds only on plants

nectar sweet liquid found inside flowers

nutrient substance that is taken in by an animal or plant to help it grow

photosynthesis process where plants make their own food using water, a gas called carbon dioxide in the air, and energy from sunlight

phytoplankton tiny plants that float in the sea

pollen special dust made by plants that is needed to make seeds

predator animal that kills and eats other animals

prey animal that is hunted, caught, and eaten by another animal

producer living thing that produces food for others to eat and does not eat anything itself

species kind of living thing; members of a species can breed to make more members

territory animal's hunting ground

toxin poison produced by an animal or plant

venomous poisonous

zooplankton tiny animals that live in the sea

Find Out More

Books

Meinking, Mary. Predator vs. Prey series. Chicago: Raintree, 2011 –
Crocodile vs. Wildebeest
Lion vs. Gazelle
Polar Bear vs. Seal
Tarantula vs. Bird
Wolf vs. Elk

Stewart, Melissa. *Deadly Predators* (National Geographic Readers). Washington, D.C.: National Geographic Kids, 2013.

Web sites

www.ecokids.ca/pub/eco_info/topics/frogs/chain_reaction/play_ chainreaction.cfm
This web site allows you to build two food chains. It then explains what happens if any of the links in the chains disappear.

science.howstuffworks.com/life/food-chain-videos-playlist.htm
This site has videos explaining various food chains and food webs, and the producers and consumers that they contain.

www.seaworld.org/animal-info/sound-library
You can listen to the gibbon and the grey wolf in this collection of animal sounds.

Index

adaptations 12, 14, 15, 18, 25
alligator snapping turtles 21
ambush 20–21
animal numbers 29
apex predators 7, 9

barn owls 6, 7
bats 15
bees 27

capuchin monkeys 5
carbon dioxide 10
carnivores 7, 11, 21
cheetahs 14
chipmunks 4, 5
clans 19
communication 16, 17, 18
competition 14, 16–17
consumers 11

decomposers 7
defenses 5, 13, 22–27
digestive systems 5, 19

eagles 23
echolocation 15
energy 4, 6, 9, 10, 12, 18
extinction 28

flower mantises 20
food chains 6–7, 8, 9, 10, 22, 28, 29
food webs 8, 9, 10, 25, 29
frilled lizards 26

gibbons 16
giraffes 12
groups, hunting in 18–19

habitats 5, 8, 9
hawks 4
herbivores 7, 11, 23
herds 24
herring 25
hoverflies 27
hummingbirds 12, 13
hunting 14–15, 18–19
hyenas 19

jellyfish 9

lions 23, 24
lynxes 28, 29

nutrients 4, 6, 7, 10

orcas 18
owls 6, 7, 11, 22

packs 19
pandas 5
photosynthesis 10
phytoplankton 9
plants 6, 7, 10–13
pods 18
poison arrow frogs 27
pollen 13
porcupines 23
predators 4, 5, 7, 8, 9, 11, 14, 16, 18, 20, 22, 24, 25, 27, 28, 29
prey 4, 5, 9, 14, 16, 20, 21, 26, 28
producers 11

rabbits 22
robins 17

scent marking 17
schools 25
seals 18, 29
sharks 9, 29
shells 23
skunks 27
snowshoe hares 28–29
species 7, 8, 12, 15, 16
spiders 21
spines 23
stings 27
Sun 6, 9, 10

territories 16, 17
tortoises 23
toucans 12, 13
toxins 27
turtles 12, 21

wasps 27
waxwings 11
whale sharks 9
wolves 17
woodpeckers 15

zebras 24
zooplankton 9, 25